A Tangle of Otters

A Tangle of Otters

Ian Saint-Barbe Anderson

illustrated by

Gabrielle Bordewich

LUTTERWORTH PRESS
Guildford, Surrey, England

First published 1984

To

OUR PARENTS
WITH ALL OUR LOVE

ISBN 0-7188-2616-7

Text copyright © 1984 Ian Saint-Barbe Anderson

Illustrations copyright © 1984 Gabrielle Bordewich
and Ian Saint-Barbe Anderson

Text set in 12/15 Plantin

Printed in Great Britain by
Butler & Tanner Ltd, Frome and London

Contents

Acknowledgements

My thanks are due primarily to naturalist and wildlife education-alist David Chaffe of Weston-super-Mare. Over a long period he allowed me hours of close contact with captive otters who, though not tame, were willing to tolerate my presence, and the facility to photograph them inside their enclosures. Without his help I would not have written this book.

I also feel very grateful to Vincent Weir, who runs the Otter Haven Project, and to his field officers, Dr Elizabeth Lenton and Dr Elizabeth Andrews, with whom I visited many otter habitats while photographing for the Project. I was given constructive criticism by Dr Andrews and Rob Jarman, of the Somerset Trust for Nature Conservation, who helped me to avoid any scientific errors in my observations.

Kate Nicoleau and Helen Duffey spent days of their precious time on my behalf typing out reams of manuscript – and I am most grateful to them.

Last, but by no means least, I would like to thank my wife, the artist Gabrielle Bordewich, and our children Callum and Katie – who spent many a damp day investigating rivers and ditches the hard way – from the water – with me, and added their own observations to mine.

My wife's drawings and paintings of the otters are a reflection of the visual side of our shared experiences, and say as much about the otters as all my words.

Ian Saint-Barbe Anderson

Foreword

'There she goes,' said Bob, as we crouched even lower in the reed-filled ditch. It was nearly dark, and we had been waiting in anticipation on this north Norfolk marsh for some hours. Bob, a local fisherman and man of the marshes, had been watching the otter bitch with increasing regularity since early autumn as she prepared to find her potential breeding holt; occasionally the dog would return too, but for the most part the discovery of her secret places had been due to a careful plotting of her feeding habits. This had eventually enabled him earlier in the day to show me the particular points at which she would heave herself out, dripping wet, to survey her territory before sliding back into the still waters. That evening, a tell-tale bursting of bubbles on the surface was going to be the last we saw of this shy, elusive and beautiful creature.

Since that autumn evening I have tried with varying success to watch wild otters, on the River Teifi in mid-Wales and in the Inner and Outer Hebrides. I have always thought of my first sighting as 'beginner's luck' – and did so again some twenty years later when the wheel came almost full circle and I heard on an October evening the faint calls of the first otter cub I was to breed.

By then, the otter – that great wanderer so shy of man – had become very rare in the British countryside, so rare that the re-introduction of captive-bred animals back into the wild, initially in Suffolk, had already been successfully carried out through the good work of Philip Wayre's Otter Trust.

The 'Tangle of Otters' story, written so emotively by Ian and illustrated so beautifully by Gabrielle, was initiated because they became close to my otters, grew to know their intimate characteristics, and were introduced through them to all the problems that otters face in the wild. Ian has moulded his story around their personalities and Gabrielle has recreated in a visual form their magic.

All of us hope that the otter will return to survive, at least in limited numbers, in the most suitable of the habitats still remaining in these islands – it will never become a common animal again, but through all the various conservation work being carried out, and with the contribution of this book, the lonely river banks and marshes of the Somerset Levels, or the windswept peat bog of Tregaron in mid-Wales, may again echo to the piercing calls of courting otters as part of their 'sounds natural'.

I hope to contribute to that story by breeding even more otter cubs to prepare, perhaps, for future re-release schemes. We have now bred four times – most recently, just days ago, the birth almost coinciding with the writing of this foreword. As I handled one of the twin cubs, just hours after its birth, all the marvellous memories of that first wild otter bitch on Salthouse Marsh some twenty years ago, came flooding back.

David Chaffe
Spring, 1984

Chapter One

THE EXCITED CLAMOUR of barking dogs drifted along the river towards a bitch otter, lying in the broken crown of a willow tree. She was stretched out in shallow sleep, invisible to all but an overhead gull which soared high on sliding outstretched wings. Half a kilometre away the dogs ran with hurried purpose as they quartered the banks. The raucous shouts and high staccato hollers of the men as they urged the dogs on mingled with the assorted barks and yelps of the pack.

The dozen or so men were strung out, spanning the river and its banks. They searched above and below water, probing every hole and root cavern with long sticks. They wore waders and stout boots. Their rough and ready garb matched the coarse flavour of their guttural encouragement to the dogs. The apparently casual way in which they moved was belied by their searching eyes, narrowed against the dancing light from the river. They were mostly farmers, tough weatherbeaten men, well used to hard physical work. They were on the river in order to clear out mink, which had been reported there for the past few years in increasing numbers. Several of the farmers had lost poultry to the mink, and foresaw a growing problem as the population of predators increased.

They had with them a motley collection of dogs. The leader of the pack was a lurcher belonging to a local farmhand. The dark-coated dog resembled a heavily built greyhound. His acute sense of smell and bursts of speed were matched by his cunning

and his keenness of eye. His followers consisted of an assortment of farm dogs and mongrels. They shared a common toughness and stamina that were the pride of their owners. A grey-coated, wall-eyed border collie was second in command. Too unreliable for use with sheep, he had a savage streak that fitted him perfectly to the role of hunter. No less fierce were the terrier-crossed mongrels whose razor wits, sharp teeth, and exploratory instincts took them into each and every hole in the river bank. Together men and dogs presented a formidable threat. The noise made by the men as they splashed and shouted was nearly drowned by the cries of the pack as they swarmed over the banks.

The bitch otter's sleep in the willow was shattered as the hunt came within three hundred metres of her. She raised her head, saw the advancing shapes of the hunters, dark against the bright green banks and sparkling river, and dropped from the willow into the river below in a crash dive, thrusting her body fast under the water away from the hunt. She surfaced after three minutes, and could still hear the dogs. She dived once more and sped away in haste. The urge to flee drove her on. She surfaced again, in the reeds this time, and listened. The breeze still carried the sound of hollering and the barking of the dogs; she dived once more and hastened down the river.

A small stream flowed into the river, and the otter turned aside to swim up it. After filling her lungs on the surface once more, she continued swimming underwater in the depths of the stream. She put two kilometres between her and the dogs and then found a hole whose opening was below water level. She swam in and surfaced deep beneath the bank. Climbing out onto the damp earth of the cavern which formed a holt, the otter lay

alert, straining her ears for any sound of pursuit. She stayed tense for a further thirty-five minutes, listening for the muffled sound of dogs from the ground above, and only when this time had passed did she relax enough to sleep once more.

The dogs had been trained to track mink and did not follow the otter's scent. In any case, her long underwater escape had broken the trail. She had been hunted before, and knew that she must stay underwater as long as possible until her fur became so waterlogged as to make it dangerous for her. She could not know that otter-hunting had been banned the previous year, or that the packs of men and dogs that still combed the river were no longer in pursuit of her.

She wondered whether her mate was close by. They had roamed the river together for the past three years. Although his range was twice as large as hers, and he had another bitch on the adjoining territory, they shared a pair bond that was lifelong. They frequently met and spent a few days together, before parting to go their separate ways once more. The bitch had been in season at their last meeting, and had successfully mated with the dog otter.

She fell to fitful uneasy sleep for the rest of the day. At dusk she swam out of the holt to emerge on the far side of the river, behind some overhanging branches. She tuned her ears to the sounds of the dusk, and pointed inquiring nostrils into every corner, from which small breezes eddied as they bounced off the trees and the banks of the stream. Satisfied that no danger threatened, she hunted for eels, catching several. Then she moved downstream to rejoin the river, and swam rapidly away to a different part of her range, anxious to put distance between her and the pursuers who had driven her on during the day.

Chapter Two

THE OTTER swam downriver to the low-lying moor known as The Levels. Once marshland, it had been drained hundreds of years before to form water-meadows between dyke boundaries. The ditches, known locally as rhynes, cut up the landscape like a pattern of hedges, bordering each meadow of lush grass and sedge. The patchwork of water-meadows was described by the lines of willows which edged the rhynes, and the farm tracks which ran atop their banks. The many confluences of these waterways linked a maze of channels, providing a wide variety of food for otters.

It was a warm dusk on that October evening. The faint warmth of the disappearing sun turned the tree trunks bright green and the grasses orange. The noises of the day subsided and peace dropped like a veil of mist over the water-meadows. Willows bent into darkly graceful silhouettes against the paling sky, which changed from yellows and greens to turquoise, fading to mauve greys as the last light withdrew to night.

Beneath the moonlit willows ran a drainage ditch, secreted in the landscape. Hidden by brambles and nettles growing on its banks, its surface was covered in duckweed. The thick and crowded banks were a delight to the bitch otter who roamed them that night. She moved in short humping runs, searching the air for any scent of danger, or of other otters. Her movements were ungainly as she arched her back in a loping gait, but her face, when she lifted it to the eddies of warm scent-

laden air, was both alert and beautiful. Sometimes, as she moved among the taller grasses and sedge, she stood up enquiringly to search out the source of some distant noise. She held her front paws neatly folded in, and lightly touching her chest.

She stayed up for only a moment, her inquisitive instincts overcome by her fear of discovery. Dropping down again, she made her way along the bank close to the water, where the sedge ran down into the ditch. Flattening herself at the water's edge, she scrabbled in the mud at the base of the waxy reeds. She felt with her hands – for in truth they were more like hands than paws – for crayfish among the reed roots, and quickly found some. Taking them in her forepaws she bit noisily into the shells, relishing the succulent meat inside. She was eagerly searching for more when her movements startled a little owl in the willow above her. It shrieked in alarm and ruffled its feathers.

The otter shot upright. Looking over her shoulder into the tree she saw the fluffed-up shape of the owl, and relaxed at its familiarity. She resumed her search for a meal but took only half a dozen crayfish before she grew tired of them. She decided to move on. Her nose and whiskers touched the water, which barely moved as her rounded smooth body slid under it, entering silently a world in which she felt secure. Her hunger had been dulled, and though it would return shortly, she was happy to nose her way slowly down the rhyne.

She moved through the water with a lazy grace which contrasted sharply with her lumbering gait on land. She brushed aside underwater weeds and floating scraps of wind-broken willow, rising for air so quietly that she hardly disturbed

the duckweed. Seen from above, her whiskery face, bright eyes and neat ears looked comical as they dripped with waterweed, under a piece of broken reed aslant her domed head.

Having taken in enough air to last her for several minutes, she disappeared under the green dots of duckweed, leaving a faint bobbing swell on the surface which showed where she had been. Air slipped from her layered fur and out of the puckered corners of her muzzle. A watcher in the moonlight might just discern an occasional bubble breaking the surface of the rhyne in the patches of clear water between the weeds, to mark her passing.

Later that night she was aware that her hunger was returning. Now she propelled herself purposefully with her powerful rudder and became thoroughly alert. She watched the water ahead for any sign of disturbance. Her whiskers were highly tuned to sense the slightest vibration in the water denoting the presence of eels or fish.

Suddenly she nosed aside a rotting branch lying on the mud. An eel slid out – quickly it turned to evade her – just as quickly she pirouetted under full power to stream after it. Closing in fast from below, she grasped it firmly in her jaws. Above her, moonlight flickered on the surface of the water, and she headed for it, keeping the struggling eel clenched between her teeth. Big bubbles escaped from her partly opened mouth till she broke surface.

She clambered onto the bank, looked around her for a moment, quietly scenting and listening, and then settled down close to the water, beside a rock. She lowered the writhing eel to the ground, put both paws firmly on it, to one side of her mouth, and proceeded to bite off its head. She champed noisily, smacking her lips, relishing the delightful taste for a moment, before she systematically bit into the body. She ate with eyes tight shut, seeming to squeeze the most enjoyment out of every crunching bite. Every few minutes she stopped to test the air for disturbance, but none came, and she was able to finish the meal in peace. Then she got up, wiped her mouth on the grass with a sideways rolling movement, and sat alert for a moment before slipping back into the rhyne.

She caught several more eels and then decided that she had eaten sufficient to keep her, and the embryo cubs in her womb, satisfied for the moment. Enough was enough: she felt it was time that the evening should provide some entertainment. She stretched on the bank, shook her paws, and then rolled vigorously to dry her fur. Squirming on the big tufts of grass, inching her body sideways around a clump, she squeezed off the water trapped in her outer fur. Then she began to run along the bank, twisting, scurrying, pausing to listen to the night, and rushed full tilt into the water once again. Thoughts of her last meeting with her mate, when they had pursued one another riotously, raced through her mind.

She twirled in the moonlight, somersaulting backwards and twisting round again to surface. Suddenly she noticed a piece of broken twig, roughly textured, floating past. She lunged at it, coming up from underneath, and grasped it in her paws. Then she began to circle underwater, rising for air occasionally and creating a swirl of mud around her. Eventually she tired of the game and went hunting again, searching the ditch for frogs or more eels – or even a waterfowl, should one be less than perfectly hidden in the reeds.

She spent about two hours of that night alternately hunting and playing. Finally she swam slowly down the rhyne, looking for a place of safety in which to sleep. She stopped to investigate several small holes in the bank, left by water voles, and then came to a dense clump of blackberry bushes that trailed from the ground above, out over the water's edge. The brambles concealed a dry path up the bank into the fastness of the prickly keep, and the otter climbed out of the water to the dry bed of old leaves and twigs hidden at the heart of the clump.

Chapter Three

AS DAWN BROKE, the otter awoke to the bubbling rising call of a curlew. She stretched lazily, stood up and shook her fur to settle the folds which had ridged in her sleep. She lifted her head and sniffed in different directions. Satisfied that nothing unusual was about, she slipped under the brambles and down into the cold wet rhyne, eager for her breakfast. She appeared later on the far bank with an eel.

As she reached the top of the bank, she saw the spiky shape of a young fox about a hundred metres away. It was silhouetted against backlit dew-sparkled trees. Its dark shape was framed by arching willows on either side of a farm gate. The fox stood still, its brush out straight, its head pointing forward and its legs astride in mid-pace as it caught the musky scent of the otter. It was painfully thin, probably recently weaned, and not yet very successful as a hunter. The otter huffed sharply, then spun around and down the bank into the water with a great splash. She swam underwater for a minute and a half, emerging silently, more cautious now; only her nose and eyes showed as she surfaced under an overhanging willow branch which trailed into the water.

A few minutes later she came across the spraint of her mate, only minutes old, placed upon a stone emerging from the earth by the water's edge. Cows came down here to drink and had trampled away the bank with their great weight and repeated visits. A little further down, the rhyne was joined by another ditch, and a very fresh spraint had been placed on a tussock of grass on a small path which connected the two ditches. Sensing her mate's nearness, she called for him, whistling a high penetrating call which was answered almost immediately from further down the rhyne.

The dog otter moved confidently towards her, swimming with his head above water to catch her calls, and in a few moments they were reunited. They exchanged scents, nuzzling one another's heads and moving in unison, delighted to be together once more. Three weeks had passed since their last meeting, and five weeks since they had mated.

They dived for eels, catching several and eating them on the bank. When they had finished eating, they wiped their mouths dry. The bitch otter suddenly grabbed hold of the dog's tail and gave it a playful bite. She then turned and ran, and he raced after her. They started a furious game of tag, up and down the bank, in and out of the water, moving as one. Shadowing each other they twisted and tumbled through the still waters of the rhyne, making them boil and bubble and slop wavelets up the bank. Never slackening speed for an instant, they spun in a cloud of water droplets which flew from their fur. They dashed around tree trunks and chased through the reeds, flattening the vegetation around them.

After a while they tired of the game and swam lazily down the rhyne in convoy. The time was approaching for the bitch to have her cubs and it was becoming more urgent to find a holt in which she could safely give birth. As the sun topped the banks and illuminated the shady rhyne, the otters knew it was nearly time to hide up for the day and nap away the dangerous hours of full light. They found a large old willow with branches which

hung heavy and low. It was a massive tree, and one main branch had split and kinked before dropping into the water. Within the split branch was a hollow big enough to conceal several otters. They settled snugly into it, sleeping back to back for an undisturbed four hours.

A passing tractor three fields away woke them with its puttering sound. The dog slipped out into the rhyne and went on his way, but the bitch curled up for more sleep. She was beginning to feel quite tired with the extra weight in her womb. As she slept she was engulfed in rising currents of warm air which invaded her sleep, reminding her of the summer past, with its buzz of insects orchestrated by droning bees and dragonflies, and the twittering chatter of the martins as they swept the fields for flies at grass-top level. The bitch snoozed in the warmth, never deeply asleep but with her defences at low level, resting muscles and nerves alike. She knew that sleep would come once she found a suitable holt.

That evening she searched the banks and nearby thickets, never quite satisfied with one or another aspect of her finds. At last she came to a place where the ditch passed a distant farm. Willows had been planted close together on one bank, with a high overhang of alders, brambles and nettles on the other. This profusion of growth hid an old holt, dug out in years past, with its entrance behind alder roots whose earthy stronghold had been washed out by successive winter floodings of The Levels. The holt was just right: deep in the bank, it sloped upwards to avoid rising floodwater. It had a dry interior cavern in hard clay soil. The otter knew she had only two or three days before she would give birth, and she started to construct a bed on which to have her cubs. She began collecting twigs which she set on the dry upper level of the holt to provide drainage for the inevitable wettings the bed would get as she entered from the water. That night and into the early morning she covered the bed with reeds torn by her teeth and carried in mouthfuls up into the holt, where they were pushed and pawed together to make a litter.

By first light the work was mainly done, and after a hasty breakfast she rolled herself dry and curled up on the bed, settling to deep contented sleep in preparation for the birthing.

Her sleep was abruptly shattered by a roaring, squealing, clanking noise which rose and fell in explosive bursts, accompanied by a stinging grey cloud of unburnt diesel exhaust which eddied up into the holt. On the bank above her a great dark shape had lain silent and unthreatening through the night; now it was awake, and roaring as though the end of the world had come.

The otter lay head up, alert yet frozen into immobility by sheer terror. The ground rumbled and shook around the holt, which shed mud from its roof. It was the choking fumes that suddenly drove her into action. She shot out of the holt into the water, scything her rudder with maximum force to propel herself down the dark rhyne. The adrenalin pumped into her system by the trauma was unleashing power and responses that she did not normally need. Behind her, the dark shape's outline ponderously changed as big mechanical arms lifted a bucket from the ground and caterpillar tracks swung the excavator round to start the overdue job of clearing the rhyne of weeds and its banks of their undergrowth. The farmer whose land the rhyne drained had been meaning for some time to unclog the rhyne and had left the machine parked ready for the job. He did not notice the dark shape of the otter fleeing from her holt.

She moved fast upstream, in danger now under the glare of full daylight. Dogs barked nearby and a car thundered overhead as she slipped beneath a bridge. A heron flapped into the sky at her passing. Astonished coots paddled furiously for the reeds or dived below the duckweed. The otter was too frantic to consider food and swam on strongly, searching for another holt or a stretch of water with better cover. The banks along here had all been stripped clean by the excavator some days before.

Gradually as she swam further upstream the banks became more crowded again. Soon the rhyne divided at a fork, narrowing as the banks closed in at last, and ash and alder shut out the harsh spotlight glare of the autumn sun. She slowed by a grove of trees where the stream was oily dark, reflecting the brightly berried cascades of bramble, honeysuckle and wild rose-hips that scrambled over each other, tumbling down one bank into the water. Ash and alder shaded and lined the other bank, offering roots and mud as cover for the otter.

Soon she struck lucky. A tree had grown out over the water to the point where it seemed it must fall in. Its clawing roots clung to the muddy bank like the strong fingers of a giant hand. The bitch dived under the roots looking for a hole, and found one. She enlarged it, digging away the soft mud until eventually she reached the heart of the old tree which was full of rotted crumbling dusty wood. She scraped and scoured a space big enough to accommodate her and her cubs, clawing back into the mud at the base of the tree and upwards into its soft centre. At last she was safe, and had no rival to claim the holt. She rubbed herself dry, and slept.

That evening she awoke from an undisturbed sleep refreshed, and with a great sense of urgency that she must complete the preparations to the holt quickly. She made again a bed of twigs and reeds, and then lay down to rest. She slept only occasionally that night and fed in the reeds on freshwater crayfish.

Early in the morning she became restless. At first, her figure had not been noticeably affected by the cubs it contained, but recently her belly had seemed at last to swell. She fussed and whimpered, rearranging her bed, getting up frequently and trying to settle her body snugly. Within an hour she felt pulsing pains in her body, and after a while she began to move gently about, panting a little. Then decisively she squatted over the bed as though sprainting, and dropped her first cub - a dog. Two more followed in the next hour, another dog and a bitch. When she had bitten off their cords and cleaned them up, she settled to sleep. Her body and tail were coiled tightly around the cubs, hugging them close and protecting them with her furry underside. Her head lay to one side and the tip of her tail met her nose to complete the circle. Her hind legs were lying along her flank, as was her fore paw, ready to stuff any upward crawling cub down again into safety.

The cubs themselves were inert at first, but as the hours wore on they felt hunger. They searched for their mother's nipples and were nosed towards them by her. And so began the first of many days spent in suckling, being cleaned, and sleeping, while their bodies grew.

The days stretched to a month before the blind fumbling cubs opened their eyes. It was another fortnight before they could walk. Until then their mother had been able to leave them for brief periods of hunting, knowing that they would not crawl far, but now they were becoming noisier and more frantic in their attempts to wander and explore beyond the confines of her body. They were now subject to many sensations from the outside world, and when they smelt the food she ate, they chittered excitedly.

Whenever a cub got half clear of the protective curve of her body and tail, the otter would

extract a paw, place it firmly on her offspring's head, and thrust the offender back into safety. If it had got too far over her body for her paw to reach, her head would nudge it back. Sometimes she grasped a straying cub firmly in her jaws, holding it by the scruff of its neck, and dropped it back into the well of her body. The firstborn cub was more inclined to adventure than his brother or sister, and his mother found his escapes increasingly difficult to contain.

Very occasionally the otter left her cubs briefly to spraint and to straighten her tired body, but she was never able to stay away for long and the calling of her cubs inevitably drew her back inside. After each feed she would lick their rear ends to make them defecate, and would consume their spraint in order to keep the holt clean and free of the smells which might attract predators. She was always careful to make her own spraints at some distance from the holt.

As the cubs grew stronger she could no longer contain them within her grasp. They began to wander a short space from her. By now she was sore and tired, but she was never allowed to rest since they constantly needed retrieving. She knew that they would be drowned if they got to the water, as they were not yet strong enough to swim, nor was their fur sufficiently developed to be buoyant.

Chapter Four

THE TIME HAD COME when the mother was forced to move her cubs to a larger and safer holt. At dawn one morning she fed them and then let them tire themselves out trying to escape her. Then, as they fell asleep, she picked them up one by one and dropped them in a hollow at the very back of the holt. She pushed the bedding in a heap in front of them to keep them warm and contained. The three cubs curled around one another, their bodies comfortably entwined in each other's tails, and slept.

Their mother slipped quietly out of the holt and climbed the bank into the alder grove. There she began to search systematically for a tree with washed-out roots or for a cavern of sorts. At the back of the grove there was some higher ground with a bank leading up to it. Among the rocks and roots was a hole opening into the remains of a badger set. The otter ventured cautiously inside, and finding it to be completely abandoned, went back for the cubs.

She picked up each drowsy cub by the loose skin above its shoulders and carried it to the new holt. The first cub called miserably as he was dropped down and left on his own. He only quietened when his brother was dropped next to him shortly afterwards. Their protesting sister was also conveyed to join them. They wriggled and jostled each other until they were comfortably wedged up against their mother, making a complete tangle of otters.

The cubs slept for three hours, during which time they seldom moved. Occasionally, though, one cub would sleepily stir, to ease the stiffness in a limb. They slept with their legs jammed tightly against one another's close-packed bodies, and their tails wrapped around their neighbours. A subtle change of position by brother or sister would trap and numb a companion's paws. Then, to the accompaniment of soft complaining murmurs, the sleeping cubs would roll slowly over, seeking a new position which was secure and warm. Their legs and tails would grope slowly inwards, waving like the tendrils of a sea-anemone, until they encircled one another again, or burrowed back into warm fur.

The cubs remained comatose throughout, but their mother slept more lightly and when they stirred would raise her head enquiringly and test the air for scent or sound of danger. Reassured that her cubs were the only cause of her wakefulness, she lowered it once more, slowly expelling the air, taken in so anxiously, with a long soft sigh.

During these disturbances it was always the big male cub who ended up at the bottom of the tangle, acting as cushion and bedwarmer for the other two. Consequently it was usually he who started the pattern of rearrangement, which ended with them all comfortably wedged against their mother's stomach, encircled by her paws and tail. When she left her cubs sleeping and slipped out of the holt for a brief spell of hunting, the cubs noticed the lack of embracing warmth and woke up. They disentangled their limbs, yawned and stretched their way into wakefulness, and bumping and stumbling began to explore their new home.

The holt was deep inside the bank, and its entrance was set at an angle to the main chamber, concealing it from view. Small spider-webs glistened with condensed water droplets in the dim light. The walls were buttressed in places by strong tap roots and slabs of rock. From the vaulted earth roof hung hairy tendrils and white strands of roots. Long scratches in the bigger roots showed that the chamber had originally been dug by badgers, with openings which led upwards to the field behind the bank. The farmer had found and closed the set, blocking its entrances with large stones. It had remained sealed up and empty for several years, until repeated flooding washed away its riverside wall.

Thoroughly well concealed, the new holt was ideal: set well back from the water, it was partly hidden by brambles and nettles on the damp bank above it, and shielded from

airborne predators by the canopy of alder branches and the blackthorn bushes around it.

By the time they were eight weeks old, the cubs were weaned from their mother's milk. She left them regularly for short bursts of hunting, feeding their ever-demanding appetites with eels from the rhyne nearby. The cubs' teeth were sharp as needles, and their muscular jaws were growing daily stronger. They chewed enthusiastically on the pieces of eel and fish brought to them by their mother, and any cub bit hard at a brother or sister who dared to attempt a little theft from its kin. Mealtimes became more quarrelsome as the cubs grew in strength and confidence. They were growing at a tremendous pace. The eldest and greediest male was wreathed in rolls of fat which wrinkled down his legs and made him look as though his coat was far too big for him. As the weather got colder their muzzles were sprouting a fine forest of whiskers, more delicate than their mother's and very dense.

The weeks went on into mid-December. The cubs lost their fine whiskers and started to grow a second set of stouter adult ones. Flurries of sleet and snow occasionally swirled round the alders, and sudden gusts of wind invaded the body-warmed comfort of the holt. Till then, the clammy cold of misty damp air had laid a chill blanket on them all, but had not prevented their mother from hunting.

All this was about to change.

Chapter Five

THE LONG NIGHTS of December slipped quietly into early January. There was little sign of life on the moor now. Not a creature ventured out except to search for food.

The wind moaned over the empty spaces rustling the few dry reeds it had not yet flattened. Rooks flew at all angles to the winter wind, which nearly knocked them out of the sky at every wingbeat. Flocks of gulls showed white against the castles of pale grey snow-laden clouds as they wheeled and screamed in the air above The Levels. They had been driven inland to avoid the salt spray that was storm-tossed against the cliffs and beaches in furious gusts. Seeking each other's warmth, half a dozen wrens shared a nest underneath the ivy. In summer they sprackled abuse at each other in bursts of harsh metallic song, but now their common need to survive drew them as close as possible.

In mid-January there was a catastrophic change in the weather. Overnight the wind, which had been flinging gales from the north-west, suddenly swung north, then north-east. Icy air moved down from the Arctic, picking up moisture as it crossed the North Sea. It arrived as a blanket of smothering, freezing fog, which roared in at storm speed. It iced up every drop of water on the plants and trees, then blasted their shapes into weird and beautiful patterns of crystals. The ice encased everything it struck.

As dawn broke it revealed a landscape of stark white beauty, and death. Creatures too weak to resist the icy blast had frozen to the ground under its savage and unrelenting force. Touched by the first light of the sun, the trees became a tracery of white twigs seen against the dark clouds piled grey on the horizon. Rose-hips and red hawthorn berries were encased in ice, like glowing stones in a diamond setting. Bracken and cow parsley heads, long turned golden brown, now gleamed inside their ice prisons, set alight by the rising sun.

The wind had not slackened, and soon the sparkling landscape turned grey under the advancing blanket of snow. The sun was blotted out as the wind dropped, and huge snowflakes began to fall. The lull was short-lived and the raw wind returned to build up razor-edged drifts tipping hedges and tussocks. A full blizzard now covered The Levels. The wind was so strong that nothing could move against it. The air was filled with minute particles of wind-blasted ice and chilled any living creatures it caught, making their bones ache. The cattle, unlucky enough to be left out on the moor, shrank into the shelter of hedges or banks and were half-covered by drifting snow within minutes. The otters and all the earth-dwellers of the moor were safely below ground. The wildfowl found shelter where they could, in hollow trees or deep in the reeds. Many died that day, unable to find a refuge proof against such ferocious cold. The gale tore at the earth and everything on it, and raged in the snow-splattered sky for twenty-six hours. As suddenly as it had come, it gentled to a sighing icy breath and departed.

That morning in the early light the hunters emerged onto a frozen deserted land, to fill their aching bellies with warm meat. The otter stepped out into the deep snow under the alder grove. She moved onto the iced-up rhyne and started searching the banks for movement, getting colder and more hungry as she went. Her paws were sore from the sticky ice. She was quietly returning to the grove, crossing a branch that jutted out into the rhyne among the reeds, when she discovered a coot frantically trying to run flat-footed along the ice. She leapt forward as it lurched sideways, missed it, and skidded to a long halt. Then she turned, and delicately, without slipping, moved back towards it. The coot was doomed, as it could not get enough speed to escape and could not seek refuge by diving. In a few controlled high-stepping movements the otter had it in her mouth, and was headed triumphantly for home. She moved with the coot's broken neck in her jaws and its body

slung over her shoulder to lie across her back.

The cubs were awake and calling for her when she arrived back at the holt. She looked quickly before approaching, in case any passing fox had heard them, and then went in to quiet them with a meal. The cubs were now in high spirits and barged their way past each other to get out of the holt and explore the snow.

Over the weeks they had worn away a slide which was their method of coming down the bank in a hurry. Now it was covered in snow. The cubs hauled themselves up by the roots of the hawthorn bushes which formed a low hedge at the top of the bank. They flung themselves onto the top of the slide to go skittering down in a tangled rush. They repeated this manoeuvre until the snow was packed hard. They were now travelling on a surface of ice crystals. They still stuck very close to each other in this new and exciting game, seeming to need the reassurance of physical contact. Once more they all set off together down the slide, and their mother watched contentedly for a few moments, before deciding to join them. She collided with them in a heap at the bottom of the slide. The cubs emerged shakily from holes in the broken surface of the deep snow. They began to shiver with the damp on their coats. Their mother noticed the change and huffed a warning to follow her back to the holt.

There the cubs rubbed themselves dry on the bed, squirming and wriggling amongst the straw to squeeze out every last drop of melted snow. Then they curled intricately around each other, intertwining legs and tails till it was impossible to tell whose limbs belonged to which animal.

Chapter Six

THERE WERE OTHER DAYS that winter when the cold was so penetrating that the family needed all their combined warmth to stay healthy, even in the enclosed holt. Though they often went hungry for a day or so, the weather was never too bad for very long, and they were able to get out on most days. They hunted the ditches for eels or the reeds for crayfish. Easily found meals were in very short supply.

Snow-bright February days gradually gave way to the sometimes warm, sometimes chill, winds of March. The smell of spring on warm mornings alternated with the blustery cold gales of retreating winter. The cubs were four months old now, able to move very fast and to chew with real effort. Their bites as they played with their mother had become intolerably painful. Occasionally she bit back with equal force, and so they learned to restrain their new-found power. At first they blundered into everything, but as they suffered the pains of indiscriminate enquiry, they learned caution.

The big dog cub was the strongest, and usually the first to investigate any new situation. His initial lesson in pain was all the more humiliating since it was on home ground. The otters were now occupying a holt under an ancient fallen blackthorn bush which had keeled over, its twisted roots and trunk spreading across the ground and its suckers taking root around it to form a thicket.

The cubs were chasing each other outside the holt. They were running full tilt around a stump, each mischievously trying to bite the tail or nip the flank of another. The leading cub was going so fast that as he turned to clear the corner of the stump he lost his footing. A foolish expression, somewhere between anxiety and fright, flashed over his face as he rolled and bumped sideways and outwards. His legs were grabbing at the air for purchase as he rolled upside-down, and buckling under him as they made fleeting contact with the ground.

When he stumbled, the young bitch made a tremendous effort to stop. She skidded on the smooth grass, leaning back on her hind legs which she forced into the ground to slow her. But the big dog was now right behind her and flew straight into her, flattening her as he did so. He was catapulted into a somersault, nose first, over her small hard body. He did two quick forward rolls and was brought up short to a particularly painful halt by the blackthorn bushes at the mouth of the holt. Blackthorn spikes are both long and exceedingly sharp. He felt hot flushes of pain as the needlepoints dug into his side and back. He screamed in rage and pain, sending the other cubs rushing for cover in alarm. He rolled clear of the bush and shook himself from whisker to tail tip as though drenched in water. Then he went quietly into the holt to lie down. He was able to pull out most of the thorns with his teeth. His mother came to him and nosed him with her delicate muzzle, pulling the remaining spikes free. He licked his wounds regularly and they recovered in a few days.

Most of his experiences were much more pleasant. He felt the power growing in his muscles and learned with increasing skill to hunt and fish. He and the other cubs spent hours stalking the ever-watchful rabbits with their young. Nose down, they searched the tussocky grasses for ground-nesting birds, and they patrolled the streams for fish and eels.

The bitch cub was seldom in danger as she was the most hesitant. She hung back from anything new, then crowded into her brothers' flanks for comfort. When frightened, she would shrink back into the nearest cover.

Once she nearly came unstuck because of her preference for concealment instead of flight. A young buzzard was drifting over the moor when she was ten weeks old. He spotted the movement of the cubs in the sedge below, and saw two of them shoot into a knot of brambles. The third cub, though, moved back to slide under a tussock of coarse grass. The buzzard decided to attack, and dropped down on rushing wings to scoop the young bitch

from the ground in its strong talons. The bird thrust down his wings at full power to lift himself and his prey clear of the ground. The cub let out a torrent of spitting screams which startled the inexperienced buzzard into releasing her at once. The drop to earth was less than a metre, and the cub landed on her feet and shot into the cover of the brambles.

The buzzard's strong claws had gripped the cub's back like a vice, puncturing the skin on either side of her spine. She was filled with sensations of searing pain as the initial shock wore off and the full force of the wounds reached her senses. She went to her mother, shivering. The bitch otter comforted her with gentle attention, licking the blood from her fur where it had welled from the punctures. Gradually the cub quietened down, and eventually settled to fitful dream-invaded sleep. She quivered and moaned at intervals, curled up against her mother's flank.

Like her brother's, the wounds soon healed and were forgotten in a rush of spring sensations. The earth had a new scent by mid-March, the smell of fresh growth, announced by the kingcups and marsh violets which grew at the base of the rocks and among the moss-covered roots of the alders. The cubs romped in a world made new.

Chapter Seven

THE MOOR, which had been flooded, was now drained to let new pasture grow for the cattle. The clank of machinery and mutter of distant tractors began to be heard as the farmers prepared for spring pastures and summer crops.

Some weeks earlier the mother had allowed the cubs to follow her out of the holt and had encouraged them to make the transition from land to water. The eldest dog cub had readily gone in after her, but the others had held back. She nudged them gently towards the water, but they ran out sideways. Eventually, she and the eldest cub went fishing, leaving the other two alone on the bank. The younger cubs ran to and fro at the water's edge calling plaintively. The bitch dived with the eldest cub and reappeared on the far side of the rhyne with a fish in her mouth. She shared it with him and they ate with great relish. The other cubs teetered uncertainly on the far edge of the rhyne until the young bitch, overcome by the juicy scent of fresh fish, dipped first her whiskers, then her body, into the rhyne and dog-paddled across, bobbing like a cork.

Left alone, the young male had no option but to follow. He did so, calling anxiously and paddling frantically until he found he could swim with ease. He reached a fallen branch which led him up to the far bank to rejoin the family. As they emerged from the water the cubs looked like drowned rats, their soft fur turned to wet spikes. However, they rolled on the grass, drying their fur and restoring it to good order.

They grew in strength and skill throughout that spring. Food was in abundance now, with ducklings, coot chicks, frogs, water voles, young rabbits, and an explosion of new life both above and below the water. They began to take pleasure in the sheer speed with which they could chase and twist after anything that caught their inquisitive fancy.

They played a great deal with each other, learning the skills they would need when they left the protection of their mother. They bit, and dodged, and pursued each other at full speed in their games. The chase now took place as much under water as on land. They streamed after leaves which swept past in the river currents, thrusting their way through the water with strong rudders at a pace which would fleetingly outstrip a fish. Their excitement in the underwater world showed in every movement of their play.

Now they knew nothing but joy, relishing the abundance of food, the hot sun and cool water, the fragrance of spring-fresh wild flowers, and the ease with which life could be enjoyed. If nothing else moved they chased their tails, whirling in a hopeless effort to outmanoeuvre their own bodies.

During the early days of April their mother led them on short explorations. Occasionally she showed them the overland short cuts which she used between water-channels. One of these ran past a track which led to a distant farm. Above the track was a hedge, rooted in an old stone wall. The track was gated at intervals. One of the lichen-covered wooden gates rested on huge iron pivots set in a pillar of stone, which was supported by the wall. Over the years the stones flanking the pillar had begun to crumble, forming small sloping rock piles. The rocky fastness behind the post was a favourite haunt of stoats.

The family of otters was ambling along the ditch which drained the path when the mother spotted movement ahead. She froze, instantly copied by the cubs. Just beyond the gate a pair of stoats were chasing each other with total concentration. The track surface here was sculptured, carved into pits of dry mud by the rain puddles, and walled by the steep-sided ruts of huge tractor wheels. The stoats went flat out down the ruts, over the sides and around the lip of a puddle crater, streaking back up the ruts once more. They moved so fast that the white bibs on neck and chest flashed up and down over the mud walls like pulses of light. The mad dance was their preliminary to courtship. They were so intent on one another that they did not notice the still otters. Like a whirlwind they spiralled gradually

away, raising pink dry dust as they went down the track like a rolling wheel. They disappeared under the tall grasses that fringed the stone wall.

The otters moved forward, catching the musky scent of the stoats as they passed the long grass. Suddenly one of the stoats stood up, looking over the grass-heads. He saw the otters and screamed abuse at them, then shot into a hole in the bank. The otters took no notice and continued their journey.

After thirty-five metres the track crossed a rhyne by means of a low stone bridge. The structure was hardly more than a drain built of stone, and the water nearly reached the top of the arch. Beside the bridge the otters slipped down a grass-walled run into the rhyne.

Chickweed choked the surface. The weed spread from clumps of reeds which grew along the rhyne's steep banks, fastening their roots into the silt trapped by fallen debris, and forming islanded knots in the water. Four otter heads dived in succession under the chickweed, their trailing tails momentarily leaving multiple lines in green dots.

Below the weed was a dark green world. The suspended particles of mud glinted dully in the few rays of light that penetrated the carpet above. On either side reed stems rose like ribbons from the oozing mud, textured with sticks and leaves, which formed the dimly lit floor of the rhyne.

As the otters swam under the bridge through the dark water they recorded their surroundings and each other's movements through the vibrations of their whiskers. Emerging from the arch the mother otter, who was in the lead, felt the wave pattern of paddling feet ahead of her.

A moorhen was swimming across the rhyne in front of her.

The otter shot through the water and took a leg firmly in her mouth. She dived down to the muddy bed of the rhyne, pulling the moorhen with her, and held it down while it struggled fruitlessly to escape.

In a short while the bird's air supply was exhausted and it lay limp in the water.

The otters took the moorhen onto the bank, and after their mother had eaten her fill the cubs hungrily finished up the scraps, leaving only claws and beak to show where they had been.

Chapter Eight

THROUGHOUT APRIL AND MAY the family was on the move as the cubs discovered the extent of their mother's range. One dawn in early May they were hunting on a stream which ran through a small wood, tumbling down towards The Levels below. The wood itself lay in a bowl of hilly fields, topped at its head by moorland, whence the waters sprang in a peat bog. The stream ran mostly over a bed of gravel and rocks, making its shallow way down the slope of the wood. It flowed fairly straight, occasionally cutting its way through the soft earth to get past rocky outcrops, and making small gorges where it did so. The cattle from the surrounding fields sometimes found their way into the wood where the wire enclosure had rusted away. They had broken down a muddy flat at the stream's edge where they drank.

Beside the stream, ash and beech trees were coming into life, their tightly rolled leaves poking out from the bud tips. Elder bushes and hazel grew under the big trees where the moist earth touched the stream. The ground between the trees was covered with a mat woven of low brambles, reaching up into clumps where they entwined the rotting fallen branches that had surrendered to the autumn gales.

The wood smelt of damp and spring growth. Along the shallows grew dense covers of kingcups, while primroses sprouted daintily on the moist shaded banks of the stream where it cut into the earth. Bluebells formed a rich green carpet of leaves under the ash trees; soon the stems would flower and transform the hillside into a blue haze. Young nettles and ferns thrust out new yellow-green shoots, adding to the moist earth-rich aroma that hung over the course of the stream.

As the otters entered the wood from its bottom corner, a jay flew up and screeched in raucous alarm, warning the whole woodland community of danger. The jay flew in short straight darting dashes as it paused on branches to look round and renew its outraged chatter. Its passage up the line of the stream was marked by brief glimpses of bright pink and blue as it flitted through patches of spring sunlight that came down through the trees. The otters halted occasionally to see what creatures might respond to the telltale jay, but none showed themselves.

The jay's calls died, and as they did so the wood fell quiet. The drone of bees and the pittering of the noisy stream once more provided the only background sound. Close at hand a yaffle laughed in falling cadences, in search of a mate. Far away – almost in echo – came the faint drumming of a greater spotted woodpecker anxious to let the females know that he too was available, and would like to meet them. A mouse moved among last year's dead dry leaves, making them whisper in protest at being disturbed. Then, as the otters were about to move on, a crashing in the deep leafy bed under a beech tree sounded as though some heavy-footed creature were skipping thunderously on the woodland floor. The mother otter raised her head, and saw a blackbird stomping noisily on the leaf litter in order to bring forth an enquiring worm. She huffed, sending the blackbird into musical retreat. It chack-chack-chacked its way in a low burst of flight to the nearest thicket.

The otters resumed their journey up the stream to a point where it sliced deep into the soft red earth. A tree had fallen years earlier, spanning the stream, and now wore a mantle of yellow-green mosses, while pungent fungi grew in slabs out of its rotting trunk. Where its branches trailed in the water a dam of mud had built around them, dividing the stream. The main force of water travelled down the right-hand channel, leaving a large puddle on the left-hand side, fed by occasional overflows when the stream was swollen after heavy rain. Frogs had chosen this for a spawning ground, and it was their presence that now attracted the otter family.

The young frogs had emerged a few days previously and were living in great numbers among the ferns and mosses of the grassy banks overhanging the stream. That dawn morning they were mostly in or near the stream catching the insects which inhabited the water and its margins. The otters found them just after sunrise, and fell to greedily. The frogs' instinct when presented with danger was to freeze, hoping to escape notice through their camouflage. Unfortunately the otters were not fooled by this and caught them easily. When they had sated their initial hunger they started to play with the frogs: prodding them to make them jump and dashing after them to repeat the game until hunting instinct overcame the pleasure of play and they ate them up.

Having eaten and frolicked their fill, they found a large fallen tree. The fall had torn its roots out of the ground, forming a spacious cavern underneath. Brambles had swarmed over the trunk, making it an inviting place for the otters to use as a hover for the day. The bitch sprainted on the fallen trunk and led the cubs in. They soon lay snoozing inside the bramble fortress.

A fox on his way home from the farm in the fields below caught the scent of the spraint and circled cautiously downwind of the hover. His nostrils flared as he took the full force of the smell from within and he trotted away from the tree, keeping downwind until he had left it well to the right of his path. His earth lay near the top of the wood. There he would get plenty of warning from the jays of farmers with guns coming up from the valley below, or children visiting the wood in search of primroses and bluebells.

The otters slept through the bright day, oblivious to the hum of spring activity around them except when it approached too close. The mother slept shallowly, her senses on low alert since the hover was not as secure as a holt deep in the ground.

Once a young rabbit shot in under the brambles, scared by a snapping twig, and as the nearest otter raised its head, leapt sideways, bewildered, and turned to race out again.

A lizard rustled through the dry leaves that had been swept under the tree by the fierce March winds, and scuttled away nervously as the mother otter stirred into a watchful attitude.

A family of five buzzards soared overhead at midday, circling in broad sweeps high on the up-current of warm air from the hillside. They spread their wings like fingers as they adjusted their feathers to catch the thermals on which they rode. The birds mewed to one

another, a plaintive call which rose and fell eerily. They wheeled around the cornflower-blue sky, showing dark blunt-winged silhouettes. Seen through the tracery of overhead trees, they formed an ever-changing pattern against the piles of white cumulus clouds. Their persistent mewing woke the mother otter again and she watched them through the bramble stalks. They moved in a slow ballet, coming together only to drift outwards again to the furthest corners of her vision. In time they were carried along the sky by the wind until they were out of sight, and eventually she heard them no more.

Slowly the sun moved around the wood. The shadow of the bramble bush lengthened till it traced a pattern of leaves and thorns on the short grass that dipped to the water. A breeze sprang up, cooling the earth-scented air, and the grass turned imperceptibly from green to gold. Sunlight came slanting low through the fresh green-fingered leaves of the ash trees and shimmered through the young yellow beech leaves, sent into a dance of bright spots by the evening wind.

Rabbits came out, hungry after a day spent hiding in their burrows, and began nervously to nibble the succulent grass, richer in spring than at any other time of the year. The rabbit population, which bred all year round, had produced an explosive springtime surge of young, for at this season they could feed on the rich harvest of the woodland floor and the tempting fields at its edge.

The youngsters came first out of their burrows, followed more cautiously by their parents. They sat, heads down in the grass, eating for dear life. At the slightest sound they sprang up and froze, ears high; then crouched, flattened, and waited. They resumed eating but then, still uneasy, raised their heads again, ears pricked high, to listen for the source of danger. They moved around in small jumps, testing each direction. Only when satisfied all was well did they crouch down once more to eat. Any further alarm sent them bounce-hopping, sometimes with great reluctance, to the safety of their burrows. Some of them had their holes close to the stream and it was they who kept the grass so short on its banks.

The otters had moved into the bramble patch hours earlier. They were awake and lying under the fallen tree by the time the rabbits started coming out from the earth.

The cubs became suddenly quiet as they scented prey, and waited till several young rabbits were out feeding. Then, led by their mother, they eased their way forward with the utmost patience, still hidden from direct view of the rabbits, whose scent now carried strongly to them on the evening breeze.

A large branch of the grounded tree lay between them and the rabbits, and they wormed their way up to it. The nearest rabbit sensed something was wrong and stood up, alert. The sun caught the top of his head and lit the fur. His ears glowed like red beacons as the light shone through them, outlining the dark veins.

The eldest cub saw the rabbit's head and moved over the branch, going straight for it. His companions followed suit, fanning out as they did so. The young rabbit thumped the ground loudly with one rear foot and dived for the safety of his home.

Suddenly rabbit ears shot up in profusion among the grass and several families were revealed. They all dashed in different directions as the otters arrived amongst them. Two unfortunate youngsters lost their sense of direction in the panic and were seized by the otter cubs who shook them, terrier-like, until their necks broke, then ran back to the brambles to consume their catch, tearing off limbs as they fought for a share.

Further up the wood, the fox smelt the blood, mixed with the musky scent of otter, and gave the area a wide berth as he set off for the easier pickings of the farmyard and its fields.

Chapter Nine

AS SPRING MOVED into high summer, the bitch otter took her cubs up and down the length of her range. Together they explored the reed beds where the waterfowl hid their nests, and every hole in the river banks. They searched the salt-marshes and the upper reaches of the tributaries that tumbled down from the hills. Nearly always on the move, they discovered and memorized all the hovers in which they could lie unseen. They marked their passing with spraints along their routes. These were messages to other otters that a family was in this part of the range.

One evening, the younger dog was hunting the river bank for something to play with, when he found a blue plastic sack. The wind was tugging at it as it lay caught in the brambles, making it flap. The cub huffed in alarm and jumped back, but the sack took no notice. It just lay there, rustling and moving as the breeze shook it. The cub moved stealthily forward and approached the sack. Then he dashed in, hit it with his open jaws, and shot back again. The breeze had dropped, and there was no response from the sack. The cub approached once more, testing the air with his nose, and watching the blue bag closely. He moved cautiously round it and found that the far end was open. Bolder now, he poked his head into the hole and then thrust forward, pushing his body almost wholly inside. At the bottom of the sack was a little strong-smelling liquid which he did not taste.

The sack gave way as the cub pushed it. He moved forward, freeing it from the brambles which had ensnared it. Then he was off, humping along the bank with the bag over his head. He shook it and swung it about him as his head whipped around inside it. Then he tucked in his back legs and started to twirl about, going down the bank like a blue hurricane until he and the bag squelched in an ungainly heap into the mud at the base of the steep bank.

The cub turned round inside the bag and came out forwards. The smell of the liquid clung to his fur, and he slid into the water and dived to rid himself of the odour. There were other sacks discarded on the river banks – some white, some black, but mostly blue – and he left them all strictly alone, remembering that unpleasant smell.

He and his brother and sister grew sleek and fit during those easy balmy days of summer plenty. By day they rested up in a variety of hovers. Sometimes they used the generously forked willows that leaned so conveniently out over the water, so that they could escape danger by dropping with a mighty splash into the rhyne below. They sheltered, too, in brakes of blackthorn and thickets of bramble, and behind the washed-out roots of trees that clung to the river bank. They learned to avoid the stretches of water where the dredgers worked, hating the stench and clamour of the huge machines which left them without cover of any sort.

The family followed routes across country which had been otter roads for centuries. In places their runs were broken by the dangerously bare excavations of man, and these they crossed swiftly, in fear of discovery. If the devastation was huge, they avoided the area altogether. With each passing year the farmers

became more aware of the need to modernize their farms and make use of machinery to scour the ditches. The otters' range was shrinking as it was invaded by more and more dredgers. There was increasing traffic, too, on the roads which linked the isolated farms to the world beyond the moor. But between the farms lay areas as yet untouched by progress, where the otters could still live in relative security, hunting and feeding and often spending a leisurely hour in play for the sheer joy of it.

On a July evening the otters were hunting the rhynes close to one of the small moorland communities which grouped themselves round a farm and a pub. It was a beautiful summer evening and the warmth of the day still pulsed out of the earth, sweet with the heavy smell of the honeysuckle that grew high in a nearby hedge. The rhyne ran alongside a road which crossed it on a small humpbacked bridge.

Reeds spiked the muddy meeting of bank and rhyne, and the water was spattered with chickweed. Below the weed, hidden from view, were fish. This was a spot the otters often visited to hunt. They came along the bank, unseen in the tall grass, and entered the water some thirty metres from the bridge, slipping quietly into the warm shallows and submerging to begin their search for a meal.

The mother otter led the group, and almost at once she surprised a bream basking in the warmth of water heated by the day-long sun. She seized the bream and carried it to the bank where she allowed her cubs a small share. As they grew older she was giving them less and less; they had to find most of their food for themselves, and now she sent them back to the water while she lay on the bank, wedged comfortably against an old stump, to finish her catch. She chewed on the fish, spitting out the scales with a flick of her muzzle and stopping between bites to raise her questing head for signs of danger. None were present.

A few minutes later the bigger dog cub emerged carrying an eel. He lay on the bank not far from his mother, and was joined shortly afterwards by his sister, who also had an eel, and lastly by the younger dog who carried his prey, a moorhen, proudly up onto the grass. The family ate with relish in the fading rays of the sun, which was dipping behind the reeds. Long fingers of shadow reached across the chickweed and up the bank on which the otters lay. One by one they finished eating, wiped their jaws on the tough grass-stems, and groomed their paws and fur with probing tongues.

Then with a stretch and a yawn the younger dog raised his head and looked around him with an air of boredom. Casually he rolled towards his brother, increasing speed and snaking his head back to give a quick nip to the tempting arc of tail as he passed. In a flash he was on his feet and darting down the bank. His brother, instantly wide-awake, shot after him at incredible speed. The young bitch cub blinked in surprise and then dashed after them. Their mother settled her body deeper into the bank and closed her eyes.

For about twenty minutes the cubs played with tremendous energy. Then they came out, one by one, to dry themselves on the still-warm bank. Their mother swam off upstream in search of more food, and the cubs settled to a watchful doze as the last of the sunlight was gathered in, leaving only the dimness of summer twilight.

After their nap the cubs began to stir again. The big dog cub voiced his boredom in small chattering complaints. The young bitch looked around and yawned, as if to indicate it was too soon to play again, but she knew her message would go unheeded. Her brother was already on his feet and stalking round the grass clump behind her. She glanced back over her shoulder at his stealthy approach, then angled herself upwards and forwards to shoot clear of his tail-teasing teeth. The younger dog could not resist the urge to join in. Under the scudding clouds that caught the gleam of the rising moon there began another furious game of tag.

The bigger dog cub was in the lead. He shot towards the bridge, as if intending to plunge under the arch, but instead swung to the right, racing up the bank. A car came sweeping over the bridge and round the corner towards him. He huffed and froze, momentarily blinded by its headlights, then spun round to dash for cover. The car's bumper caught him in mid-air, sending him flying. He landed on the bank with a crack of breaking ribs, frantically kicking to right his broken body. But a searing pain in his lungs stilled him, and then, quietly, he choked to death as the pierced arteries and ruptured lungs filled his life's breath with bubbling blood. His body toppled down the bank and hit the water with a splash.

The other cubs, seeing the light blaze behind his silhouette, had whirled away to fly down the bank into the rhyne. When the dead cub landed in the water, they thought it was a crash dive, and hid in the reeds. Then, as the car sped away, they emerged and picked up the scent of blood mingled with the smell of otter. Uneasy, they swam to him, nosed his lifeless form, and turned away. Twice more they returned as though to convince themselves of the reality.

Their mother rejoined them soon afterwards. She was restless all that night, waiting for her cub to return. When he did not do so, she seemed to realize that he would not come back again. She stayed close to the bridge for another day but then she and the other cubs moved on.

That summer she had slowly become aware that a part of her territory was much less disturbed than the rest, and it was to this area that she now turned. The quiet part of the moor, where no one used machines to scour the rhynes or drain them of water, was marked by a post driven into the bank. It was, in fact, a notice which declared that the land beyond belonged to a Conservation Trust, set up to protect the moor and its wildlife.

There were no plastic sacks in this area. The wildfowl seemed to know that it was a safe place and were to be found there in greater numbers, which in turn meant easier eating for the otters. People were seen occasionally, but the otters hid from them and were never spotted.

In August there was a lot of heavy rain and the rhynes swelled with floodwater, opening and scouring new holes behind the roots which clung to the banks. There were two or three days when great white clouds built towering shapes against the slate sky and hung over the hot waterlogged moor with an air of stormy foreboding. At this time the otters were sleeping in a hover under old discarded sheets of rusting corrugated iron. Around the pile of sheets had grown an impenetrable stronghold of brambles, fringed by nettles. The first clap of thunder heralding the storm resounded under the iron sheets and woke the otters at once. They lifted their heads quickly, huffing and suspicious.

Heavy drops of rain bounced on the corrugated sheeting. The otters smelt the sweet moisture-laden breeze which eddied into the depths of their thicket. Mother and cubs relaxed, in the knowledge that this was a thunderstorm and of no danger to them. They

settled themselves in a complex arrangement of intertwining bodies and slept soundly throughout the rest of the storm.

The last rolls of thunder died away as the clouds moved on over the moor. The evening light was hazy and green, catching the glistening drops of water that hung from every leaf and twig in the saturated air. Across the water-meadows birds who had been silent during the storm started to sing as they emerged from their leafy umbrellas.

The otters moved lazily against one another. They stretched each limb in turn. They yawned, forcing their jaws apart to full stretch and showing strong sharp teeth and red gullets. The mother poked her head out from under a piece of wood attached to the corrugated iron. She tested the air for danger and moved out with an inquisitive expression on her alert face. The male cub joined her at once, followed hesitantly by his sister. They emerged from the nettles down a passage of tall soaking grasses which dropped pollen on their shiny fur, where it stuck like caraway seeds on a bun.

As they reached the river bank they startled a heron who was brooding over the swollen rhyne, shielding himself from the light with wings arched over his head. He gazed down through the darkened water, ready to strike at anything moving within range. He heard the otters passing and broke the still evening with a sharp 'dzank' as he shrieked his disapproval. His long legs hinged as he lowered his body to spring into the air. With ponderous wing-beats he rose and flew a curve away from the otters, disappearing over a line of willows that marked the edge of a drainage ditch.

Ignoring the heron, the otters slid one by one into the water, to begin the evening's fishing.

Chapter Ten

THAT NIGHT the otters continued their journey down the river and across the bitch's range, until they encountered a bigger, faster river that was fed by the numerous rhynes of the moor. They swam downstream, going fast and easily, towards the edge of the range where it met the sea.

They reached the estuary at first light and crossed the salt marshes, taking the most direct line to the shore.

All along the tideline groups of waders daintily pattered the mud for molluscs and worms. Oyster-catchers, their bright patches flashing in the low light, poked their orange bills into the mud. Knot and dunlin ran over the sandbars in a zig-zag search for burrowing lugworms. Moving like shadowy frail ghosts, they criss-crossed the beach exposed by the retreating tide and fed feverishly.

An alert dunlin spotted the hump of the first otter as it topped the sandbar and was silhouetted against the dawn sky. The bird fluttered uneasily into the air. The rest of the flock stopped feeding and anxiously scanned the low horizon of the shore. Then they, too, saw the otters.

The surviving male cub moved forward first, making a hopeless attempt to rush the flock of sea-birds. In an instant the air was filled with the flash of urgent wings.

The birds rose and wheeled as one, then split into small groups seeking different directions of escape. They patterned the air with ever-changing formations as they flitted across grey

cold banks of early morning cloud. As the sun lit their bodies it caught their black backs and wings so that the flock resembled a huge smoking dark cloud.

The leaders suddenly doubled back, their white undersides gleaming in the dawn, and it appeared that a wash of palest silver was being drawn back through the swirling flock. The whirr of their wings and the sound of their high-pitched alarm calls rose above the noise of the breaking surf.

The otters took no notice of the commotion but headed for the rocks at the curve of the bay, seeking the marine life that lived among the weeds surging on the slow swell. As they entered the water the buoyant salt sea lifted them high and they bobbed among the kelp beds.

While searching the weeds the bitch cub noticed a bright ball riding the wavelets and swam out to investigate. She circled the ball, watching closely for a reaction, but it kept floating up and down on the swell, always returning to the same spot. Curious now, she nosed the ball, but it stayed, unusually, in place. She dived below the sunlit water and found a rope going straight down from the base of the ball. She spiralled down the rope, and as she saw the sea-bed she sensed movement.

A nylon rope basket hung there, with a small lobster trapped inside it. The cub approached eagerly and felt her way around and about the cage, brushing it with her whiskers until she found the entrance. She slid in through a narrowing tunnel entrance and attacked the lobster, which had no way of escape.

Having used up two minutes of air, about half the supply available to her, she decided to take her prey to the surface and eat it on shore. She turned to go out of the cage but found her way was barred.

Quickly she tried again in several other places, all in vain.

The cub dropped the struggling lobster and started to circle the cage with a sense of urgency. Her lungs were getting short of air as more and more bubbles of the life-giving element slipped past her tightly clenched teeth and up to rejoin the atmosphere.

She began to chew at the cage, trying to break out, and had bitten away two strands of closely woven rope when she felt the first weakness in her muscles. Panicking, she attacked the cage with desperate ferocity, biting in a frenzy of hopelessness.

She stopped and took a gulp of water, searching for air and finding none. She gulped again and was unconscious. One more uncontrolled gulp, and now her mouth stayed open. Her limp body opened out in a graceful curve. She drifted into the nylon which held her in its deadly embrace.

Once more the mother otter and the young male cub knew the temporary pangs of loss. They never found her body.

Within a day or two they had forgotten her. Life and its routines demanded all their attention.

Chapter Eleven

THE LATE DAYS of August were marked by a change in the weather heralding the onset of autumn. The temperature dropped three degrees centigrade. The cool winds were south-easterly, bringing skies of high grey cloud which hung in an unbroken veil over the moors and hills.

Trees which had shown the solid dark green of high summer suddenly wore small patches of yellow and rust where their earliest leaves lost their vigour and died. The hedgerows were marked by tall yellowing grasses which spiked out of the green foliage like thin spears.

The change in air temperature slowed the activity of the butterflies and set the martins fluttering as they gathered on the telephone lines, strung like notes on a stave of music.

Then in early September the cool spell lost its dampness, giving way to strong dry northerly winds. During the day the sun beat hot on the moors and rivers, charging the warm air with moisture. When the cool evening winds came to claim the day, they condensed the moisture and turned it into millions of tiny droplets, blanketing all the foreground with mists. As the sun went down, huge and red, cool fingers of mist rose out of the trees and wreaths of vapour drifted over the slow-flowing waters of the moor. Within twenty minutes the landscape was blotted from view in a smother of mist which clung clammily to every blade of grass and dripped from every twig and leaf. Silence descended on the otters' country as all but the harshest

sounds were deadened by the thick air. The bitch and her cub hunted in the swirls of mist with as much confidence as in clear air, relying on their noses and whiskers to find their prey.

By eight o'clock on the following morning, when the sun lit the mist, the otters were travelling up a hill stream to sleep. The stream ran steeply down through a wood. As the sun came over the dark gorse which topped the hill, it burst on the shrouded woods like a searchlight. The mist billowed and swayed in answer to the wind created by the warming rays from above.

Giant slivers of sunlit mist were thrown out in a pyramid shape. The otters were picked out in a shaft of bright swirling light and paused for a moment, lifting their heads to the air. Around them shafts of light splayed out from the sun. The whole area was transformed into a landscape of silhouetted trees bound together with vertically angled bands of light.

Not caring to be so conspicuously illuminated, the otters slipped into the water and continued upstream, blinking as the sun caught bank-top leaves and ferns and turned them to a yellow blaze of bejewelled fronds and splashes of light. They hurried into the shadows of their holt, which was up under the roots, half washed-out, of a big sycamore at the stream's edge. They glanced back to see pools of light, green and pale yellow, spreading on the water beyond the holt as big splashes of dew were shaken off the leaves by the dawn wind. The gleaming ripples from the splashes moved towards each other, touched, shimmered, and spread back through successive rings.

A hundred metres upstream a pair of badgers came to the water to drink, and then shuffled off slowly, nosing left and right through the undergrowth as they went. Finding a spot that suited them, they stopped and each in turn clawed away the mat

of roots and grass at its feet, making a shallow scrape in which to deposit its droppings, while the other kept watch for intruders.

A dipper at the stream's edge made its way along the bank flitting from stone to stone, and then walked down into the virgin sunlit water in search of breakfast on the bright stream-bed. It walked until it disappeared under the ripples, catching water-borne insects as it worked its way steadily upstream.

The otters slept away the hours of daylight in the holt under the sycamore. That night they went on up the hill stream, towards the heights of the moor.

Chapter Twelve

THE RIVER spanned the moor in broad reaches, but on the higher ground it was narrower, confined by rocky banks. In contrast to its lazy pace across the moor, it here moved quickly, boiling over rocky ledges, lipping into fierce short waterfalls, eddying and back-tracking in whirls over river-bed obstructions of solid strata.

The force of the river had carved out deep pools below the falls. Its banks were overhung with hazel and oak, birch and spruce. Mosses softened the rocks, and ferns sprang feather-like from the crannies split by frost in the containing walls of stone. Higher still, the steep sides were topped with heather, and rowan trees, bright with September berries of orange and scarlet, shaded the gorges which bottled up the forceful torrents below. Impatiently the roaring waters cut a gash through the land as they tore their way down to the calmer reaches of The Levels.

The deep pools below the waterfalls were rich in fish which sought their shaded depths. The otters searched them out with ease. The sheer excitement of this part of the river was something the bitch was never willing to pass up. She and her cub were fascinated by the impact of rough water on the smooth deep pools. Their sense of play led them to dawdle, bellies upturned under the jets as they tried to bite the sparkling liquid that flashed past them.

They hunted for crayfish and freshwater mussels, and chased

a large fish out of hiding below the fall. Then they climbed out of the river, making their way up the rocks. After searching a small gorge for a few minutes they found a pile of rocks against which grew a big-rooted silver birch, and eased their way into the space that opened out under the tree. They slept fitfully, eyes opening at the slightest change in the sounds which entered their rocky fastness, but lulled by the noise of the stones knocking and grumbling as they were pushed around the river-bed.

The bitch and her cub spent several days on the clear upper reaches of the river, hunting for grayling and trout, and catching them easily in waters which had been undisturbed for some time. An Indian summer was prolonging the season beyond its allotted time, delaying the onset of autumn. The smell of summer still lingered in the warm mellow evenings when the otters lay head to head in the curve of a rock pool, relaxing in the sun-warmed water. Birch and alder were starting to yellow, their leaves glowing golden amidst the green foliage of sycamore and ash.

The cub was ten months old now, almost full-grown and well able to hunt for himself. He still clung to the companionship of his mother, but every now and then a restlessness overcame him, during which he strayed from her side for a few hours to hunt and to explore the territory. Each expedition took him a little further from her as he pushed out the limits of his dependence.

Late one afternoon the cub moved off to a spot higher up the river where he had successfully caught fish on the previous day. He slid into the depths of the pool and almost at once located a grayling, silhouetted above him. He came upwards from low behind the fish, which accelerated away as it sensed his pressure wave. The cub was already moving fast and sprinted after the fish with a burst of speed which overcame it. He surfaced with the grayling held firmly in his jaws. Taking it to the bank, he ate it slowly, enjoying every crunching bite without fear of competition.

Having eaten his fill, he re-entered the river and headed downstream, investigating the banks. At one point the river met a bed of rock which turned it aside from its hitherto straight course. At the bend the bank had been eroded over the years by the constant force of the flow. The ground above sloped gently up into a wood, and the trees at the water's edge dipped their roots in the river, clinging precariously to the undercut bank. The roots

of one tree had been half washed-out, forming a deep cavern – a natural holt which had been further excavated by otters in previous years until it reached deep below the tree. It was to this rooty stronghold that the cub came as he meandered from bank to bank.

He nosed his way in, cautiously at first. Finding no trace of an occupant, he ventured inside and settled himself snugly in the deepest recess, to fall asleep.

An hour later the cub was startled awake by a muffled earth-shaking roar overhead, followed by a huge slap of water outside. Instantly alert, he became aware of an unsteady roaring sound mingled with small splashes. He ran to the mouth of the holt, choosing a position inside the embrace of the roots, from which he could see out while still hidden by the dark shadows of the entrance.

Leaves and twigs torn from the trees were hustled past by the urging wind. They fell on the flattened wavelets of the river and were blown at angles to the current in wild dancing whorls as the wind bounced off trees and rocks, seeking passage between them. Firmly wedged aslant the river, and already damming debris, lay the shattered trunk and snapped branches of an ancient ash, brought down by a sudden gale with an almighty sucking gust.

Spray was dashed into the holt, streaking the otter's fur with lines of droplets, and the roots framing his view of the water shuddered for a moment. The cub's eyes narrowed and he shrank away from the forces unleashed by the gale. He retreated to the inner chamber, lying uneasy and watchful. His nostrils flared repeatedly and he huffed his alarm in small expulsions of breath.

At length the wind abated, and with its going the cub relaxed. At about midnight he set out to retrace his route to his mother's holt among the rocks. He approached it, whistling for her. Reassured by her answering whistle, he went in.

They greeted one another, and the cub eased himself in beside the bitch, with a grunting shove of his rear quarters to wedge him tightly against her side. His tail curled over her body, and with a groan of contentment he lowered his head onto her flank.

For a few moments he gazed over her hip into the dark. Then his eyes closed, and his chin sank into her fur. He was warm and safe once more. Together the otters fell into deep contented sleep.

Chapter Thirteen

AS THEY SLEPT, the dog otter who had fathered the cubs was moving upriver, following the trail indicated by the bitch's spraints. Towards the end of that night he came to the small gorge, caught her scent and whistled a greeting which went unheard amongst the noises of the river. He moved closer to the hover in the rocks, scenting her strongly now, and called again. This time the bitch heard him and huffed in alarm, uncertain of his identity and ready to defend her hover if necessary.

The bitch searched the breezes eddying into the holt and recognised the dog's scent. Her whistled greeting floated out to him and she emerged from the holt. They moved together sideways, nose to tail, to confirm one another's scents. Then they nuzzled their heads and set off together. They went to the river to fish, leaving the cub alone in the hover.

The cub dared not venture out, unsure of his reception by the adult male. Although the big dog appeared to be friendly towards his mother, the cub held back, afraid he would be challenged. The adult otters hunted and played together for two days, during which time the youngster stayed out of their way. However, the bitch was not yet ready to be courted, and worked her way back towards her cub.

The dog otter was never far away in the days that followed. He kept checking the mother's spraints, searching for a change in smell which would indicate she had come into season. A month later he got the signal he was waiting for. The bitch had moved back to the moor with the cub and was moving slowly as though waiting for her mate. He was travelling a parallel course, and once he sensed the change in her he back-tracked her spraint trail to meet her. He found her at the edge of a field paddling for food among the roots that lined the water. They chittered joyously, greeting each other with much rubbing of heads.

The dog otter began to approach her with a view to mating. She sensed his intention and huffed a warning to keep away. Running swiftly down the bank, she leapt into the water with a splash, quite unlike her usual silent immersion. The dog followed, and there began a game of tag that took them through air and water as if the two elements were one. They tussled and shoved one another on the bank, rolled down it together, chased in convoluted circuits, each echoing the movements of their partner. They dashed out of the water, up the steep bank, round the trees and down into the river again, as though linked by a tow-rope. Perfectly symmetrical in their pattern of movement, they porpoised and spun, embraced and chased, till the water boiled and the banks were a sea of mud soaked by their furious pursuit.

They did not mate that night, but stayed together. On the following night they repeated the pattern but this time, gradually, they slowed. The dog approached the bitch more deliberately and she was less combative, as though she had worked out her aggression in the chase that preceded their coming together. Gently they joined in the water, rolling and lifting their buoyant bodies in the river's embrace. They mated in a cradle of water which slipped and sighed around them, encircling their pliant bodies.

When it was over they hunted together for a few days and then parted. The bitch moved on towards the sea while the dog went off towards the big river that cut the moor in two. They would meet again, occasionally, in the months to come. As they roamed the area, they always noted one another's spraints, adding their own to impart the information that they had passed by.

The young male otter moved away from his mother in search of new territory. Almost a year old now, he was a cub no longer, though still too young to mate. He wandered in solitary search for other young otters to give him company. The cycle of the year was about to start again, and his journey into adult life had begun.